# The Wooden Balloon - A Poetry Collection

Ellena Coxall

BookLeaf
Publishing
India | USA | UK

Presentation by *BookLeaf Publishing*

Web: www.bookleafpub.com

E-mail: info@bookleafpub.com

ISBN: 9789357446716

First edition 2022

# DEDICATION

Mum.

Who gives me everything I could ever possibly need, including endless amounts of incredible love & faith. You're my inspiration always.


Dad.

Who gave me his gifts of art & creativity.
Forever loving you.

# ACKNOWLEDGEMENT

Well, honestly I never thought I'd get here so early! I know it's only a small book, but thank you so much for picking it up and seeing potential, depth and just something within the words printed in these pages. So I guess my first acknowledgement goes to you. Thank you.

The next acknowledgement should really be the one who made this all happen & i'm so happy and privileged to give them a mention! Book Leaf Publishing, please keep doing what you do. You're inspiring young authors everywhere and giving them such incredible opportunities. Thank you.

Elizabeth Janes. You have been my constant reliance, my shoulder to cry on (even with 250 miles between us), my inspiration and my best friend.

A big part of my identity lies through my faith in God. I have such a strong group of friends, family & loved ones in Bangor, home, camp holidays and overseas that have uplifted, encouraged and walked with me through my journey with God through pain, anxiety and defeat. And to those people, I am eternally grateful. You helped me get here.

# PREFACE

Would you believe me if I said that I found this book opportunity through a link on my university course group chat? That group chat itself was lost through my spam folder, so I aren't Iglad I found it!

This collection is a variety of pieces of work that I've submitted through university assignments, one's I've already written down in my spare time and scribbled in notebooks and ones that are fresh and new! I hope you love them like I do.

'Each of you should use whatever gift you have received to serve others, as faithful stewards of God's grace in its various forms'
- 1 Peter 4:10 (NIV)

# The Wooden Balloon

The pain didn't fit my body.
                              My structure was
disembodied.
It spilled over from my twisted gut to the corners
of my lips, stretched the skin out in a beastly
manner that veins appeared from the temples of
my head and the path up my fingers.
                              Satan lingered.


It must have looked on the outside like rage.
It must have sounded like rage.

An unearthly scream emerged from my body
and flooded out from my mouth. I vomited
excessively with the noise.


My ears tingled and rang from the harsh sound
and my eyes squeezed shut so tightly like they
were being strangled
It made my head spin.

The dizziness forced my stance to become
crippled
and I crumbled to the floor like a screwed-up
piece of paper,
                                        Crippled.


Crumbled.
I bounced off the wall slightly with my shoulder
bone that would surely leave a purple stamp on
my skin later.
                                    Add to the
collection.
                                            An
inhuman selection.

Mislay protection.

Years of

privation.

My bone knocked against the cells and
interrupted the flow of my sickly blood.
                                  No sickly blood
was apparent on the outside.

But I could taste it.

My lungs were hard and stiff, no air could enter
and there was no air within

It was a wooden balloon.
                              Hollow.
a wooden balloon. I think of it being etched into
with a knife that leaves a pattern on the surface
                              Maybe the pattern of
the brain.

The lines are not too deeply cut, they wind
through one another
The wood is a dark oak
The oak you would see in a forest dressed in
moonlight

Masses of effulgence
Ready for a murder scene, don't you think?

The wooden balloon of my lungs were still
shrieking.

# A Natural Panic

B R E A T H E
Said the girl to the trees
They towered above her like large natural
skyscrapers
Some of its leaves fell in panic
She held her hand out and placed it on the wood
of the trees torso
It was rough and dry
Dry as the earth's soil below

S T E A D Y
Said the girl to the sun
It blinded her vision and sped its rays through
the gaps in the trees
It was burning her skin unintentionally
And wouldn't let any clouds hide it
No matter how fast they tried to run in front of it
The sun was too strong

C A L M
Said the girl to the stream
The water ran fast down the course as the
bubbles tripped over the rock beneath
Small waterfalls were being created in its stress
The girl ran her fingers through the water

Trying to slow the pace of the earth's heartbeat
 Until the water was still

And the forest relaxed.

# Gravestones

He sits on the worn wooden bench every Sunday
afternoon
Just beside his wife
It has been a year and he still feel she was taken
too soon
But she had a good life

Another man stands in front of another marble
gravestone with his hands behind his back
Just standing before his wife
It's been a couple of years now since things
started going dark and almost pitch black
But she had a good life

These two elderly men would sit and stand
Both in the silent company with their loves
Until one of them decided to lend a hand
Before push comes to shove

The man suffering with the most recent death
Was gifted a chair, a bench by the other man
So he could contain his stamina and his breath
When he came to visit his wife when he can

The man who was gifted the chair was warmed

By the generosity of this other grieving fellow
A smile crept upon his face when he was
informed
From there he said his first thank you to the man
and a hello

There was now two men sat on chairs
Both in the company of their wives and now
each other
Still sitting broken but content through their
prayers
Knowing that God had brought them one
another

(Based on a true story)

# The Little Church on the Mountain

There was a church that was sitting on top of the
mountain
Small and squashed with a wide brick stone wall
body and dark windows for eyes
It didn't look sad or lonely, just a little old
It's seen the high and lows of life, through
baptism, marriage, and the worn and torn faces
as their loved ones, dies.

How many elders have gone before me here?
My mother places her hand on a stone cemented
to the wall beside the entryway
Wondering how many other people have placed
their hands on that stone
How many people have leant against this wall
with their emotions struck with grief and their
tears fallen on the uneven stone below?
Their bodies shaking so much that they
depended on this wall to stand
How many brides have stepped out into the chill
of the day with their new groom?

Or how many bodies have come in and out of
the church, taken by death too soon
There were gravestones for six- and
sixty-year-olds dating back to the seventeenth
century, wobbly in their stance and hunched
down in their age

The sea and its creatures surrounded the little
old church on the mountain
Decorating it's surroundings with crystal blue
water on a good day, and an eerie fog over the
farm fields on a bad day
How many have walked the path that I took and
saw the dolphins that I saw?
How many saw the birds that fly and nest just
near the church door?
How many have walked your path before?

# Shape in the Water

I became a shape in the water

where light would bounce off my skin and travel

through the transparency

Hope for transparency

Hope for tomorrow

Hope for wondering eyes to be drowned

Words drowned

Separating of hairs

Separating of stares

The lipstick stays on

The mask still on firm

I breathe through the water

Until I feel it choking my throat

Oh what ecstasy fills my lungs

And runs through my ribs

Water hitting the bone and returning to the
current

My nose rises up for the water to be released

For I am released

I am seen to be below the sun

In the depth of aqua

But what if you are the desperate

drowning underneath,

And I the one holding you there?

# Rivers

Rivers and

        streams are

                like the

                        veins of

the earth.

They wind

and wrap

themselves over

and under

every corner

every gap

every cranny

                              and fill

                the world

with cleanliness,

refreshment and
      baptism in
         an impure

broken world.

It offers

peace of


mind and


a restored

soul made

and created

by God.
         We should
     live with
the salt
in our
   bloodstream. We
       would change
           our

perspective

on how

to treat

the earth.

Perhaps.

# The Teacup & the Teaspoon

'I hear the kettle' said the teacup to the
teaspoon, 'I feel the steam against my side'
'I feel it too' replied the teaspoon
'I am the one to feel the heat of the water first'
said the teacup to the teaspoon
'But I am the one who holds the sugar first, to
add the sweetness to their morning' replied the
teaspoon
'I am the one who is held first in her hands, she
gives me comfort, and I her' said the teacup to
the teaspoon
'But I am the one that mixes the potion, as if you
were a cauldron' replied the teaspoon, the back
of the steel stained with the tea from yesterday
'I am no cauldron; I do not gather up wicked
spells. You gather stains and rust from your poor
duty laid upon you' said the teacup to the
teaspoon
'I stain because I am used often. It is a mark of
reliance. You have no marks of reliance, just a
chip' remarked the teaspoon

The teacup replied to the teaspoon 'My chip is
small and irrelevant, I remain the favourite
teacup', the other dozens of teacups rattle in
distain behind in the cupboard.
'I complete the drink that is filled inside you.
She dances with me as I twirl around the warmth
and tap the lost drips off the top of you' replied
the teaspoon
'It causes me pain when you tap like that. But
she kisses me after with her lips against my
brim, and heals what you have caused' said the
teacup to the teaspoon
The teaspoon replied with 'I do not wish harm
against you; without you I would have no
purpose'
The teacup did not respond.

# Transparency

By the waters edge
> She sees the flood coming
towards her
> Dread engulfs
her
> Panic suffocates
her
> Until the water
reaches her
> And It doesn't
touch her
> Its close but it draws
back
> Gently kissing the stones as they roll
beneath the incoming wave
> The rocks change
colour
> When the water reaches
the stone
> Like it is carrying
paint
> It paints the rock a new
colour

                    Three or four shades lighter
than before

                              She doesn't change
colour

                              She doesn't
change

                              But she feels
different

                              Her mind is at
ease

                              The bulge in her throat
calms

                              And her breathing
slows

                    How transparent and open
the water is

                    Always vulnerable to
what's underneath

                    Exposed by its own
cleanliness

                    Or hidden by its own
pollution

                    She dips both hands in to
feel the chill
   The water feels like its seeping through her
bloodstream and hitting the bone
                    She brings them out with the
water droplets

                    Acting as decoration
alongside her rings

                              She didn't change
colour

# October

Blow a kiss
Blow away
Below and forward flow
Do the autumn leaves go

Dance and unwind
Dance dramatically
Water licks the rocks in the stream
Running wildly like a dream

Read the sky
Read the stars
Trees shake at the pushing of the wind
Sun dissolved as the moon appeared, so fair
skinned

Share a weight
Share the burden
Gravity of the rain
Puts the earth in pain

Plant an idea
Plant in the dirt
The harvest in orange blooms

Before the death of winter looms

Walk a path
Walk straight
The gravel in drunkenness itself winds
Leaving the green fields behind

Show me love
Show me yourself
In the purest white of the snow
the warmth must go

Paint what you see
Paint what you smell
The slow seeded flower only knows
Which direction the strong nectar goes

Jump as you mean to
Jump to conclusions
Nested on the wet cold surface of the lily
By God positioned unwillingly

# Green Needle

tree screams
like the painting in pain
a whistling pain
one that echoes through the hollowness of bones

bones?
sweeping through the blood flow

                      is there a
flow?

                      dirt

stamped juice from the root

             thick
             dark
             deep
              fruit

        where's eve?

hollow scream
wrinkles of bark
around the cracks of its lips
a mouth crammed of age
not a year of it spills out

three thousand and forty four

branches in sheer panic
waft and wave and weep
green needle
threaded
in the wooden
skin.

# Narnia

I looked behind every cupboard, wardrobe, and
shelf I had
But there was no door, or hole or gap in sight
Even in the library, where the books were
dressed in leather, and the curtains in blue plaid
There was no secret world or adventure that had
come to light

I ate Turkish delight in the hopes of drawing in
the white witch
The cream of the chocolate and the sweetness of
the jelly hit my teeth and dissolved on my
tongue
I wouldn't be like Edmund. I wouldn't be a
snitch
But I couldn't grasp on the magical hope for too
long

There was no chill where the snow would be
The snow that would decorate the earth on the
other side of the door
Where you would glide through the cold to meet
Mr Tumnus for tea
There wasn't even a chill in the air, so I became
less sure

I refused to believe that Narnia was a story
The characters are too real, the world too great
and the adventure too strong
I wanted to see Prince Caspian and Aslan in all
their glory
Why didn't they bring me along?

# Finding Julian

1 9 7 6

Grey marble
Yellow strike slashed though the middle
We are a green marble
Blue strike slashed through the middle
This marbles in pain
Bleeding colour ball
Marble tends to rain
Good rain knows the best time to fall,
                    don't you think?

rain talks
Speaks, calls, preaches,
Droplets dialogue discomforts
the words soak through the throat

Shouts in the S I L E N C E

Julian heard.

He was swept away from sleep
In the midst of the fog deep
Felt the mountains weep
The mountains was theirs to keep

Julian fled
Julian was taken
Julian's dead
Many are mistaken

In the peak
I believe there is air that is not air
Breath that is not breath
And life that is no longer

Arrive on time
Arrive alive
Depart only to another place
Where living is not the case

Grey marble looms over the peaks
Red strikes slashed through the snow
We are still a green marble
With no safe place to go

If Julian is still holding his stance
Up there in the peak
I want to know if there is a chance
That the rain still speaks
For I should know in advance
If I am too weak
To enter this foggy trance
Thinking I am unique

Julian will be found
If for one second,

We can block out the mountains' calling sound.

# Radio Silent

radio silence
a silent radio
a quiet wave
a small hit
lost within rain
falling rain
jumping rain
rain is causing pain
pavement in pain
road in pain
I lie on the road
Every corner of me flat on the tarmac
Grounded on ground
Damp in the puddle
A satisfying comfort
Only a road can provide
A flat one
A quiet one
An empty one
Lying in the place where death could occur
But not letting it happen
A small control over death
Creates a big satisfaction
A great adrenaline
Only a road could satisfy

In the radio silence
on the forgotten street

# Glass Bucket

Loving you is like
A glass bucket in the rain.
Damn overwhelming.

Loving you is like
A glass bucket in the rain.
Fragile and Useless.

Loving you is like
A glass bucket in the rain.
Transparent and dank.

Loving you is like
A glass bucket in the rain.
Strong and abnormal.

Loving you is like
A glass bucket in the rain.
Abundant and clear.

Loving you is like
A glass bucket in a storm.
What are we doing?

# Consume

Curled enough to kill

to strangle and to

consume

the fear I released

# How lovely to be lonely

I am loved, locked and lonely
In place
I am a safe space.

How lovely to be lonely
To be lonely next to something so wide
So overwhelmingly free
The saltiness of the sea

I am insignificant
Next to the roar of the water

Deep, dark, and deceiving
Light and bright
That's how I am perceived
strong and steady

                        I think.

I am bound by stone
Dressed in white
A bride to the island

A bride abandoned
That sits on the edge
Decorated with a black stripe
Waves reach out for comfort
Instead, they hit, and they hurt
Enter in all corners of my lower body
And violate
Accidentally
       I think.

Next time you see me
Think of me and my purpose on occasion
Before the sea and the salt make their invasion.

# Grounding

1)      Name 5 things you can see.
okay. you can do this.
                  b r e a t h e
I see his eyes looking straight at me.
widened and panicked.
wild and weary.
I see the mirror behind him
I'm wild
And I'm weary.
I look wired.
I look weird.
I see a pot in the corner of the room
Filled with wilted rustic orange roses
Their heads bowed down
Gloomy and forgotten
I see the bottle I dropped on the floor when I
started shaking
The water is now still trapped in the plastic
Watching me through the transparency
In concern, I don't know
I see the door left slightly open
The lights outside of it flickering
Even the lights are disturbed
I've disturbed everything
And everyone.

2)      Name 4 things you can touch around
you
okay. keep going.
b r e a t h e
I can feel the carpet beneath my hands
The feelings uneven
My balance in uneven
And my shaky hands quiver just about the
surface
I lift my other hand, but it's trapped
In the hands of him
Thumb stroking the top of my hand
Presenting the new sensation of warmth to my
cold skin
I can touch the wall at the back of my head
I gently rock my head back and forth
Feeling the brick
Hoping the panic wouldn't stick
I also feel the sickness
It emerges through the pipes in my stomach
And I pray that it doesn't escape

3)      Name 3 things you can hear.
almost there.
b r e a t h e
I can hear him panting
His breath is matching mine
I need him to stay calm too
I'm affecting things again

36

I can hear the lights flicker outside the door
They twitch and wriggle
And sound like little electric shocks
I can hear the cars behind my head
Above on the wall where the window sits
I hear the speed descend and ascend


4)	Name 2 things you can smell
you're doing it. you're okay.
b r e a t h e
I can smell the stench of the old coffee in the
machine
It lingers through the room
The smell stains my clothes
I smell burning
I don't know why
I don't know where
It feels uneasy in the room
Everything still feels a little uneasy


5)	Name 1 thing you can taste.
last one then you're there.
b r e a t h e
I can taste my sickly bitter blood
From biting my cheek too hard
But holding my tongue to much
The blood seeped out
and sits in the shelter of my mouth

I made it.

# Mint Lemonade &
# Green Cardigans

may fourteenth
the sun illuminated a spectacular
twenty-five-degree heat on my skin
the pale, almost translucent texture that is a sheet
for my blood
was burning, but in a good way
and it was a good day

as my skin slowly darkened by the absence of
the moon
my throat yearned for substance only mint
lemonade could fulfil
the mint leaves floated alongside the bubbles
that ran up and down the glass
created a shimmer that reflected on the grass

i swallowed slowly as the bubbles liked to tickle
the walls of my throat
the straw inserted a powerful dose of ice and
refreshment
that sometimes my teeth find unbearable

and send shock waves to the tubes of my brain
and the pink flesh of my gums
until the warmth of my tongue comes

the shade crept in beyond the tip of the trees that
danced with me all afternoon
branches waved and swayed
with the rhythm of the water, the waves, the
wind
suddenly captured the darkness in the sky
as the clouds came by

a green cardigan at hand that covered my now
tanned sheets of skin
is now buried beneath the cream of the green of
the cotton
another girl wore the same cream green
she could have been hit by the chill of the eve
or simply didn't want her skin to breathe

# Have you seen my hat?

Have you seen my hat?
I can't remember where I put it last
It fits loosely around my head
Curved around the edge and the top is flat
The back is mirrored to cast
The reflection of the dead
Flowers in which they sat,
In the bed of the soil perishing fast
The lining inside is velvet red

He's the one that placed this hat on me
From that moment I was lost
The memory is sharp and cutting
A paper edge painfully
If I had known what cost
Would I have stopped the hand from putting
His mark where I can not see
The blood made of frost
My own thoughts fast shutting

The memories are the ones I fear
Of the hours unspent and the words unsaid

I dare to put the hat back on
What if I told you my hat was near?
That it was in my eyesight as this poem was
being fed
The truths and tortures of this man that is gone
The ending of poems are meant to be clear
Have you seen this hat on my head?
As I dwell upon.

# HELP

'H' is for the hollowness inside the tree, the
habitat, the home, the hundred

'E' is for everything under the ground, the bugs,
the beetles, the buried

'L' is for the light that illuminates the forest
floor of which I'm lying on, among the leaves,
the lonely, the layers

'P' is for the problem. Also for peace. The peace
within the problem, the politics, the people. Pray
for the problem.

# Silence of the Sea

The waves stumble over one another as they came running into the shore

Tripping over each little white bubble

Letting in a big breath

Inhale.

The water sucking in the air as it pulls its lungs back

Grains of sand gets stuck in the mouth

Choking

The sea spits it back out again

Exhale.

Pushing the edge of the water back

It silences the rest of the beach

Creatures. Wind. People.

The wind tries to shush back but the water is
greater

Trees start to wave at the water

The water just breathes

How great it is to see their interaction

Nature vs nature

It pushes again

White noise, white bubbles and white foam

Rhythmically.

Repeatedly.

White noise like the static on your TV

Rustling of plastic

Now spread along the tip of the shore

Bits of plastic that once belonged to something
that was never meant to reach the sea

Choking.

Blocking the airways
Let
    The
        Sea
            Breathe.